Witness History Series

THE THIRD REICH

David Williamson

The Bookwright Press
New York · 1989

Titles in this series

China since 1945
The Cold War
The Origins of World War I
The Russian Revolution
South Africa since 1948
The Third Reich

Cover illustration: The frontispiece to the official Nazi
history book, *A New Germany*.

First published in the
United States in 1989 by
The Bookwright Press
387 Park Avenue South
New York, NY 10016

First published in 1988 by
Wayland (Publishers) Ltd
61 Western Road, Hove
East Sussex BN3 1JD, England

Library of Congress Cataloging-in-Publication Data

Williamson, D.G.
  The Third Reich.

  (Witness History)
  Bibliography: p.
  1. Germany — History — 1933–1945 — Juvenile literature.
  2. World War, 1939–1945 — Germany — Juvenile literature.
  I. Title   II. Series
DD256.5.W492   1989   943.086   88–24272
ISBN 0–531–18261–4

Typeset by Kalligraphics Limited, Horley, Surrey
Printed by Sagdos S.p.A., Milan

Contents

The Weimar Republic

THE WEIMAR REPUBLIC was formed as a direct consequence of German defeat in the First World War, followed by revolution. If the war had not been lost by October 1918 and Germany plunged into chaos by strikes and mutinies in the army and navy, it is difficult to see how the German nationalists, industrialists and generals would have ever accepted a democratic constitution. However, in November 1918 they had no choice but to bow to the storm. On November 9, 1918, a republic was declared and the Kaiser abdicated.

From the beginning the Republic failed to secure its position. It was supported by the Liberal parties, moderate Socialists (the SPD) and the Catholic Party (in the center). But it had to rely on units of the old imperial army and on the newly formed Freikorps, which were full of right-wing volunteers who hated the Republic, to defend it from the Spartakists (Communists). It failed also to fire the Kaiser's civil servants, judges and professors, who could not always be relied upon to support it.

In its early years the Republic faced so many problems that it had no chance of winning over its enemies. It was hated by the Nationalists, who could not come to terms with Germany's defeat, and by the extreme Socialists and Communists, who believed that the Weimar Republic had betrayed the revolution. It also had to accept a dictated peace from the Allies as laid down in the Treaty of Versailles, which had reduced Germany's army to 100,000 men, stripped

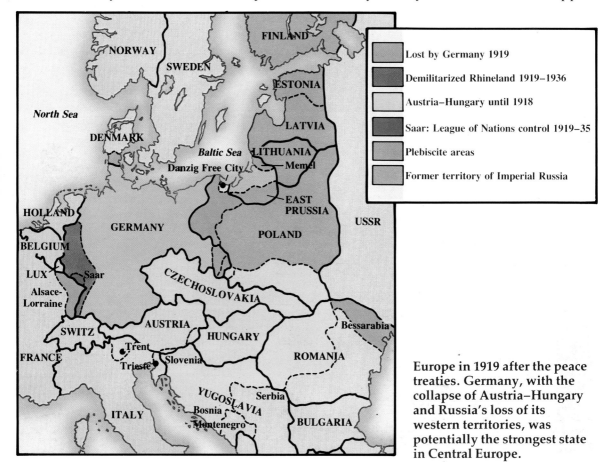

Legend:
- Lost by Germany 1919
- Demilitarized Rhineland 1919–1936
- Austria–Hungary until 1918
- Saar: League of Nations control 1919–35
- Plebiscite areas
- Former territory of Imperial Russia

Europe in 1919 after the peace treaties. Germany, with the collapse of Austria–Hungary and Russia's loss of its western territories, was potentially the strongest state in Central Europe.

▲ This Democratic Party poster charts the obstacles the Republic had overcome since 1919.

Germany of its colonies, gave West Prussia to Poland and handed over the Rhineland to an Allied occupation, which was to last for fifteen years. The treaty also committed Germany to a crushing program of reparations, which in May 1921 was finally fixed at 132 billion gold marks.

For the next four years the constantly changing governments of the Republic were too busy dealing with threats of putsches from both the Left and Right, and with pressure from the Allies for the punctual payment of reparations, to be able to restore the economy and take the necessary measures to halt the escalating inflation in the value of the mark. The origins of the postwar German inflation went back to the decision in 1914 to increase the circulation of paper money to help pay for the war. Inflation benefited the great industrialists, but destroyed the savings of the self-employed and the middle classes. It also caused great hardship for those who were on a fixed income. Inflation caused whole classes to lose any confidence they might ever have had in the Republic.

▼ At the end of the First World War German battleships were paralyzed by the mutiny in the North Sea of November 1918.

The formation of the Nazi party

In November 1918 Adolf Hitler was an unknown lance corporal with a good war record. Before 1914 he had been a loner, who could not settle down to the tedium of a regular job. He drifted around Vienna and Munich picking up the extreme racist and nationalist views that were popular at that time. In the army he found for the first time a sense of purpose and comradeship. Later he described how the news of the revolution reached him while he was in the hospital recovering from a British gas attack:

Everything went black before my eyes; I tottered and groped my way back to the dormitory, threw myself on my bunk and dug my burning head into my blanket and pillow.[1]

Hitler soon became convinced that fate had chosen him to save Germany. When he returned to his regiment in Munich in December 1918, he found a city in revolutionary turmoil. Order was only restored by

Adolf Hitler at the height of his powers as Führer and Chancellor of the German Reich in 1936. In 1920 he was just an obscure rabble-rouser, unknown outside Munich.

Spartakists (Communists) take cover behind a barricade of papers and newspaper bales during a street battle in Berlin in January 1919. Their attempts to gain power were crushed by government troops.

the Freikorps in May 1919. The army authorities exploited Hitler's fanaticism to use him as an agent to counter the spread of Communist propaganda among the troops. He attended meetings of the German Workers' Party, one of the many small nationalist and anti-Semitic groups that sprang up in Germany after 1918 in reaction to defeat and revolution. Hitler was so impressed by it that he became a full-time member.

He soon became its most dynamic member. He helped draw up its 25-point program, the key points of which were:

1. We demand the union of all Germans in a Greater Germany . . .
2. We demand . . . the revocation of the peace treaties of Versailles and Saint-Germain.
3. We demand land and territory to feed our people and to settle our surplus population.
4. Only members of the nation may be citizens of the state. Only those of German blood, whatever their creed, may be members of the nation. Accordingly no Jew may be a member of the nation.
5. All citizens shall have equal rights.[2]

The party soon changed its name to the National Socialist Workers' Party (or Nazi for short), so that it could attract both Socialists and Nationalists. Hitler organized its propaganda, and was its most effective public speaker. Thanks to his contacts with the army Hitler raised money to buy a newspaper for the party and set up the S.A., which protected Nazi rallies from being broken up by Communists. In July 1921 Hitler was strong enough to take over the party leadership himself, and by 1922 the party was one of the leading nationalist groups in Bavaria.

The Ruhr Crisis and the Munich Putsch

In 1923 Hitler's chance seemed to have come. The French occupied the Ruhr in January in response to German delays in paying reparations. The German government responded by encouraging a policy of passive resistance among the workers, which was financed by printing even more paper money. This inevitably led to uncontrollable hyperinflation. At first public opinion supported the government, but in September the new Chancellor, Gustav Stresemann, was forced by the collapse of the mark to negotiate with the French. This led to a revival of unrest in Germany. Communist revolts were prevented in Saxony and Thuringia, where the government sent in troops and used emergency powers under Article 48 of the Weimar Constitution to restore order.

In Munich Hitler played a key part in setting up a coalition of the extreme nationalist groups in Bavaria. His plans for a victorious march to Berlin, where he believed that he

In January 1923 French troops occupied the Ruhr, Germany's leading mining region.

could bring about the collapse of the government, could work only if he won the backing of the authorities in Munich.

At first this seemed possible as both the State Commissioner, von Kahr, and the head of the local garrison, General von Lossow, were convinced that the Republican government in Berlin was about to collapse. But they changed their minds once Stresemann restored order in Thuringia and Saxony. This provoked Hitler into staging the notorious Beer Hall Putsch of November 8. With 600 of his S.A. he surrounded the *Bürgerbräukeller* where Kahr and Lossow were addressing a public meeting. He proclaimed a national government and forced them into supporting it. Unwisely Hitler then let them go, only to find that on the following day they ordered the police to bar his march into Munich.

▼ Stacks of fifty and twenty-million mark notes, each worth only a fraction of a pfennig (penny), waiting to be paid out as wages in 1923.

▲ The accused in the Hitler–Putsch trial, 1924. Hitler, looking defiant, is standing between Röhm and General Ludendorff.

Sixteen Nazis were killed and two days later Hitler was arrested.

With several other Nazis Hitler was tried for high treason, but he was able to use the publicity given to him by the media to turn the trial into a propaganda victory for National Socialism. Hitler told the judges:

> . . . it is not you who pronounce judgement upon us, it is the eternal Court of History . . . That Court will judge us . . . as Germans who wanted the best for their people and their fatherland, who wished to fight and die. You may pronounce us guilty . . . but the Goddess who presides over the eternal Court of History . . . acquits us.[3]

After such an appeal it is not surprising that the judges, who had no love for the Republic, only sentenced Hitler to the minimum period of five years' imprisonment.

Hitler rebuilds the party 1924–29

Hitler was released in December 1924. He found his party banned and its members deeply divided. The political situation was also unfavorable for him. The mark had been stabilized, and the adoption of the Dawes Plan by the Allies and Germany led not only to a French evacuation of the Ruhr, but also introduced a more practical program for reparation payments. The German economy, helped by loans, particularly from the United States, began to recover.

Despite the changes in the political atmosphere, Hitler was determined to rebuild his party. His priority was to keep control over his own party. He was not going to join any more alliances, as he had in 1923, unless he was unquestionably the leader. He also decided to work within the constitution by campaigning for Reichstag seats until such a time as he could legally create a dictatorship by forming an elected government. First he had to reunite the party, which was split between those who wanted to see the Nazi party become more socialist with greater appeal for the workers, and those who supported Hitler's more nationalistic approach. The party was refounded in 1925 and within a year Hitler had re-established his control over it by building up his image as the all-knowing, all-powerful Führer. In

This Nazi election poster calls on the voters to destroy "the World Enemy" – Jewish high finance – by voting Nazi.

Hitler in the Landsberg prison with (from Hitler's left) Maurice, Kriebel, and the future Deputy Führer, Hess. The pleasant surroundings indicate that as political prisoners they were treated with leniency. In fact, Hitler was released after serving only nine months of his five-year sentence.

1928, Goebbels wrote about Hitler:

We are all convinced, so that our conviction can never be shaken, that he is the mouthpiece and pathbreaker of the future. Therefore we believe in him. Beyond his human form, we can see in this man the active grace of destiny.[4]

The party's headquarters in Munich were reorganized and a Reich Directorate was set up to strengthen Hitler's grip on the party. The Gauleiters were given responsibility for building up the party in their areas, but also made strictly accountable to Munich. The S.A. was re-created in 1926, and over the next four years an increasing number of professional and youth organizations were set up, such as the Hitler Youth and the Women's League. Over the period 1925–29 Hitler had created what one historian calls "a framework for the future of the mass party."[5] Hitler succeeded in absorbing most of the other extreme right-wing groups, and therefore by 1929 he alone spoke for the extreme Right.

The Weimar Republic collapses

THE WALL STREET CRASH of October 1929 had a devastating impact on Germany because much of its economic recovery since 1924 had been financed by short-term loans from the United States. As a result of the Crash, the Americans now needed this money themselves and therefore began to recall it. Consequently a large number of German businessmen went bankrupt or let many of their workers go. This was the main reason why the depression in Germany was far more severe than it was elsewhere. Unemployment rose dramatically as these figures show:

Year	Number of unemployed in millions
July 1928	1.012
Jan. 1930	3.218
Jan. 1931	4.887
Jan. 1932	6.042
Jan. 1933	6.014[6]

The crisis also affected German politics. The Great Coalition, which had been in power since 1928, broke up in March 1930 because its members could not agree on a package of cuts. Heinrich Brüning, the leader of the Center Party in the Reichstag, became Chancellor. In September he called an election in the hope of strengthening his position, but he succeeded only in giving Hitler a chance to campaign in conditions that encouraged the extremist parties. It was not surprising that the number of Nazi seats in the Reichstag shot up to 107. Thanks to the backing of President Hindenburg, Brüning remained in power and governed with emergency powers under Article 48.

In May 1932 Hindenburg was persuaded by General von Schleicher to fire Brüning and replace him with Franz von Papen. Schleicher, who was in charge of the political and press affairs of the army, was impressed by how Hitler had polled 30 percent of the votes in the presidential elections of March 1932, when he had stood as a rival to Hindenburg. Schleicher felt that Hitler should be brought into a coalition government. Von Papen was considered more likely to be able to negotiate successfully

Unemployed workers lining up up to collect unemployment benefits during the depression.

The Nazis appeal to the workers in the election of March 1933. The poster reads: "Our last hope: Hitler." In fact, the Nazis failed to win over a significant number of the working classes.

with Hitler, but first he tried to strengthen his own position by going to the polls in July. The Nazis won 230 seats, and von Papen failed to persuade Hitler to join his cabinet. Von Papen therefore had no other choice but to call yet another election, as he had little support in the Reichstag. He also hoped that he would be able to wear the Nazis down.

Although in the November election the Nazis lost 34 seats, it was clear that von Papen would have to go. On December 2 he was replaced by Schleicher himself, but he too failed to trap Hitler in a coalition. The way was now open for von Papen to negotiate a deal with Hitler, whereby Hitler would lead a Nazi–Nationalist coalition, but would be heavily outnumbered in the cabinet by non-Nazis. Von Papen convinced Hindenburg that Hitler would be safely under control, and so he was made Chancellor on January 30, 1933.

The figures below show the Reichstag election results in Germany from 1928 to 1933, in terms of the number of seats gained by each of the parties. The Nazis won most of their seats by taking votes away from the Nationalists (DNVP), the right-wing Liberals (DVP) and the Democrats (DDP). The moderate SPDs and the Center Party managed to maintain most of their share of the votes.

Seats gained in Reichstag elections 1928–33

	1928	1930	1932 (July)	1932 (Nov)	1933
NSDAP (Nazi)	12	107	230	196	288
DNVP (Nationalists)	73	41	37	52	52
DVP (right-wing Liberals)	45	30	7	11	2
Center (Catholics)	78	87	98	90	73
DDP (Democrats)	25	20	4	2	5
SPD (Social Democrats	153	143	133	121	120
KPD (Communists)	54	77	89	100	81

The Nazis exploit the depression

The depression enabled the Nazi party to pick up the protest vote from a wide cross section of German society. The Nazis won the majority of young nonunionized first-time voters, an ever-increasing number of small businessmen and self-employed workers, many white-collar workers, such as teachers and office workers, as well as a large number of small farmers, who were suffering from the worldwide fall in agricultural prices. They also presented themselves as the attractive alternative to socialism to the industrialists and to many of the upper-middle classes.

The Nazi party managed to attract the support of so many different groups whose interests were often contradictory to each other with the help of its very efficient propaganda machine. It was organized centrally at Munich, but each party regional area and

A small store forced to sell-up by the depression. The notices announce that "The advertised prices are no longer valid. We will accept any reasonable offer." This became a common sight throughout Germany during the early 1930s.

branch had its own local propaganda office. The Nazis concentrated on each group separately, promising them an end to their misery. The young and the unemployed were promised work, the farmers higher prices for their crops, and the small businessmen and the self-employed protection from the ruthless competition from chain stores or large-scale industry. Through rallies, films, leaflets and intensive canvassing, the Nazis spread their message. According to one senior Nazi, Otto Strasser, Hitler was by far their most effective weapon:

14

[He possesses] an uncanny intuition, which infallibly diagnoses the ills from which his audience is suffering . . . [He] enters a hall. He sniffs the air. Suddenly he bursts forth. His words go like an arrow to their target; he touches each private wound on the raw, liberating the mass unconscious . . . telling it what it most wants to hear.[8]

This clever exploitation of discontent made Hitler an extremely effective politician. However, it explains only part of his success. Hitler also united these different groups by appealing to their common German nationalism. The Nazis stressed that they were a classless nationalist party that would help all Germans recover their self-respect. One upper-middle-class woman in Hamburg wrote in her diary:

Every person who thinks and feels as a German, the bourgeois, the farmer, the prince and the intelligentsia, stands by Hitler. It is the nationalist movement.[9]

But the Nazis were unable to win much support from those groups that already had their own organizations and traditions. They failed to win over the Catholic regions of southern and western Germany or the great mass of the working class, which was unionized and voted either for the SPD or the KPD.

▲ A 1933 poster claiming massive support for Hitler. The slogan runs: "Yes, Führer, we will follow you." It conveniently ignores the fact that only 43.9 percent of the German population voted for him.

▼ Hitler addressing the Reichstag on May 17, 1933. Goering presides and the Nazi deputies give him the Nazi salute. Hitler has just given his famous "peace speech," in which he claimed that Germany was the only country to have disarmed itself completely.

Could Hitler have been stopped?

We have seen that Hitler had built up a party that was able to exploit the crisis created by the depression. His plan was to gain power legally, but it was not easy for the Nazis to win an outright majority in free elections. Commenting on the seemingly spectacular Nazi gains of July 1932, the British Ambassador in Berlin remarked:

> *Hitler seems now to have exhausted his reserves. He has swallowed up the small bourgeois parties of the Middle and the Right, and there is no indication that he will be able to effect a breach in the Center, Communist, and Socialist parties.*[10]

The table of Reichstag election results on page 13 confirms this assessment of Hitler's position in July 1932. When Hitler failed to become Chancellor after the July 1932 elections, opposition to his policy of legality from the S.A. threatened to split the Nazi movement wide open. In August after Hindenburg had vetoed a Hitler government, Goebbels noted:

> *The S.A. leaders assemble at the Command of the Chief of Staff. The Führer and he give them a fairly full outline of events. Their task is the most difficult of all. Who knows if their units will be able to hold together? Nothing is harder than to tell a troop with victory already in their grasp that their assignment has come to nothing!*[11]

The election results of July 1932 had given the S.A. good reason to feel victorious.

A German cartoon of 1932 showing the Communists, the Nazis, the Roman Catholic Church and the Socialists lining up to fight both the Weimar Republic and each other. Had either the Catholics or the Communists cooperated more closely with the Socialists, Hitler's rise to power might have been blocked.

A police water cannon driving Nazi and Communist demonstrators from a street in Berlin on June 27, 1932. Such rioting was frequent throughout the years 1930–33.

The Nazi attacks on the von Papen government during the autumn election campaign and their support of the Communist-inspired transportation strike in Berlin frightened off many of their middle-class supporters. Thus the election results of November 6 seemed to suggest that Hitler's tactics had failed: the voters were beginning to desert him, party morale was declining and the financial contributions from businessmen were falling off. Within the party Gregor Strasser, who was in charge of party organization, now believed that Hitler should compromise and join a Nationalist coalition. Schleicher tried to split the Nazis by offering Strasser himself the vice-chancellorship in the cabinet, but Hitler vetoed it and only Strasser's grudging obedience to the Führer held the party together. Later Strasser openly criticized Hitler:

There are two paths which can lead to a solution of this serious crisis . . . the legal or the illegal path. I would be prepared to follow either path. But I refuse to wait until the Führer is made Reich Chancellor, for by then the collapse will have occurred.[12]

With support for the Nazi movement declining and conflict arising within the party, Hitler may have been on the way to "the rubbish pile of history."[13] But he was saved when von Papen produced his plan for a coalition with Hitler as Chancellor.

Hitler secures complete control

AFTER HIS APPOINTMENT as Chancellor Hitler's immediate aim was to secure complete power. He persuaded his cabinet to call yet another election as he wanted to win a convincing majority, which would allow him to create a dictatorship, while claiming that public opinion was behind him. His campaign was helped by the Reichstag fire, which appeared to have been started by a half-witted Dutch Communist, Van der Lubbe, but in reality was quite likely to have been the work of the Nazis themselves. It gave Hitler the excuse to issue emergency decrees enabling the police, on orders from the government, to arrest and detain individuals as long as they liked, to censor the mail and to search private houses.

Despite these advantages, the Nazis gained only 43.9 percent of the vote; but with

On March 23, 1933 the Reichstag debated the Enabling Act in the Kroll Opera House. It was finally passed, opening the way for Hitler to assume dictatorial power over Germany.

the help of the Nationalists, who won a further 8 percent, Hitler could just claim to have won a majority. The next step was to persuade the Reichstag on March 23 to pass the Enabling Act, giving him full dictatorial powers for four years. As the Weimar Constitution could only be changed by a two-thirds majority of the Reichstag, Hitler had to use a mixture of intimidation and violence, carried out by the S.A., and top-level negotiations with the Liberal and Center parties, to push the Act through.

Once the Reichstag accepted it, Hitler was legally free to impose Nazi rule on Germany. By the autumn of 1933 only the presidency, the army and the Catholic Church were still free from Nazi control. Hitler set up a Lutheran *Reichskirche* with a pro-Nazi priest as a bishop. The political parties, the trade unions and the local state governments were either dissolved or brought under Nazi control by the process known as *Gleichschaltung*.

In 1934 Hitler strengthened his position still further. In a dramatic purge he removed many of his old critics from both inside and outside his own party who were showing too much independence. In the "Night of the Long Knives" on June 30, Röhm and the main S.A. leaders, as well as Schleicher,

Gregor Strasser and many others, were murdered. Von Papen himself only narrowly missed assassination and was hurried out of Germany as Ambassador to Vienna.

Hitler was thus free on the day Hindenburg died (August 2) to combine the offices of Chancellor and President and to become the Führer of Germany. Even the army no longer maintained its original aloofness and took the oath of loyalty to Hitler in gratitude for the elimination of the S.A.

Needless to say, by 1937 there was no question of Hitler's giving up his dictatorial powers!

The Reichstag (German parliament) building burning on February 27, 1933 after being sabotaged by the Nazis. The destruction of the Reichstag, which was blamed on the Communists, marked the end of the Weimar Republic.

The Enabling Act

Von Papen was so confident that he had effectively harnessed the Nazis to a Nationalist government that he boasted:

> *What do you want? I have Hindenburg's confidence. Within two months, we will have pushed Hitler so far into a corner that he'll squeak.*[14]

But something went wrong; Hitler slipped the leash. Von Papen later explained why it had happened:

> *My own fundamental error was to underrate the dynamic power which had awakened the national and social instincts of the masses.*[15]

This painting by the Mexican Diego Rivera, done in 1933, shows Hitler as the master of a culture based on violence.

On August 2, 1934, the leaders of the armed forces of the Reich swore allegiance to Hitler. Throughout Germany troops were paraded to take similar oaths of loyalty.

Many Germans welcomed Hitler's appointment. To those frightened and depressed by the last three years he seemed to be a savior who could unite the country. This feeling comes across in the diary of Frau Solmitz, who was a Nationalist rather than a Nazi:

> Torchlight procession of National Socialists and Stahlhelm! A wonderfully elevating experience for us all. Goering says the day of Hitler's and the nationalist Cabinet's appointment was something like 1914, and this too was something like 1914.[16]

Those who did not approve of this type of unity were subjected to a campaign of terror from the S.A., which, after the Reichstag fire and the election, at times seemed to be out of control and to threaten

Hitler's image of the "legal revolution." It was, however, important to maintain this image because it confused Hitler's opponents and won the toleration of important groups in Germany such as the army and the industrialists. It was, therefore, vital for the Reichstag to pass the Enabling Act. A combination of promises and threats were used to ensure that the non-Nazi parties did not refuse Hitler the two-thirds majority support he needed in the Reichstag to pass the Act. The Center Party was persuaded by promises of concessions to the Catholic Church, and the Communists were already in prison. The SPD was subjected to pressure. One deputy later described the scene:

> When we Social Democrats had taken our seats . . . S.A. and S.S. men lined up at the exits and along the walls in a semicircle.[17]

Nevertheless they had the courage to vote against the Act, but Hitler still achieved his two-thirds majority by 441 votes to 94.

Hitler consolidates his position

Even though Hitler had now had full dictatorial powers for four years, in April 1933 there were still powerful groups that could have stopped him. The trade unions that had defeated the right-wing Kapp Putsch in 1920 were intact, as was the army, the presidency and the political parties. Nevertheless, Hitler was able to destroy every rival center of power within the state except for the army and the presidency by the autumn of 1933. His success was not due just to terror but also to the spell he continued to weave over Germany. His propaganda, speeches and appeals for unity, which could be heard by millions over the radio, gave the impression of an irresistible revolution, which in spite of some outbursts of S.A. brutality, was basically a positive force that

▲ Hitler's dramatic style of speaking was one of his greatest strengths and gave him an extraordinary power over the majority of Germans.

▼ The massive scale and impressive pageantry of Nazi rallies were shows of strength intended to impress both Germany and the world.

Hitler speaks to assembled masses in Vienna 1938. He had managed to rise from poverty and obscurity to a position of power.

would lead to the revival of Germany. On May 1, for instance, a day before the trade unions were abolished, Hitler preached national unity at a rally in Berlin:

> *We want to be active, to work and make brotherly peace with one another, to struggle together, so that some day the hour will come when we can step before Him [God] . . . [and say]: "Lord, You see we have changed . . . the German nation has once more grown strong in spirit, strong in will . . . now bless our struggle."* [18]

This rousing speech was obviously designed to win the support of German workers.

Hitler's charisma was not the only reason for his success. His potential opposition was also divided and over-optimistic about its chances of surviving a Hitler government. The Nationalist Party, the industrialists, the army, the Catholic Church and even the trade unions, which were demoralized by high unemployment and by the intimida-tion of their leaders, thought at first that they could appease the Nazis and maintain their independence. Hitler was also careful not to unite his enemies by allowing revolu-tion to go too far too fast. He did not want Röhm's plans for a new people's army and the ideas of the party's economic sections for breaking up the big chain stores and industrial trusts to frighten the generals and industrialists into opposition or to damage plans for re-armament. A week before all the non-Nazi parties were abolished, Hitler called a meeting of his Reich governors and told them:

> *The revolution is not a permanent state of affairs, and it must not be allowed to develop into such a state. The stream of revolution must be guided into the safe channel of evolution . . . We must therefore not dismiss a businessman if he is a good businessman, even if he is not yet a National Socialist . . .* [19]

As long as Hitler kept expressing this kind of tolerence, the generals, the Nationalists and industrialists would not consider it worth their while to work together for his overthrow.

The Röhm affair, 1934

By the autumn of 1933 Hitler appeared to be securely in power. Then in 1934 he faced a real crisis, which could have destroyed his regime. Hitler's refusal to support Röhm's plans for turning the S.A. into a revolutionary people's army had caused much resentment among both party veterans and S.A. leaders. Röhm for instance openly complained:

> *Adolf is a swine. He will give us all away. He only associates with the reactionaries now . . . Getting matey with the East Prussian generals . . . we've got to produce something new, don't you see? A new discipline. A new principle of organization. The generals are a lot of old fogeys. They never had a new idea . . . I'm the nucleus of the new army, don't you see that? Don't you understand that what's coming must be new, fresh and unused?*[20]

A clash between Hitler and Röhm was likely, but the situation was further complicated by the growing impatience of the generals with Hitler's failure to discipline Röhm quickly. They feared that Röhm would push Hitler into a second revolution, more inclined toward the Socialists, that would finally sweep them away. As Hindenburg was dying by the summer of 1934, there was a real possibility that all the remaining non-Nazi forces might insist on the restoration of the monarchy and that would block Hitler's plans for combining the presidency with the chancellorship.

A cartoon in a British newspaper after the "Night of the Long Knives," showing Hitler, Goering (dressed as a Wagnerian hero) and a timid Goebbels, supported by the army, threatening the S.A. To them Röhm was a threat that had to be eliminated.

Goering, Röhm and Hitler (left to right), shown together when all three were still close colleagues.

On June 17 von Papen warned Hitler:

Have we gone through the anti-Marxist revolution in order to carry out a Marxist program? . . . Would the German people be the better for it, except perhaps those who scent booty in such a pillaging raid? . . . At some time the movement must come to a stop and a solid social structure arise . . . Germany must not embark on an adventure without a known destination, nobody knowing where it will end. History has its own clock. It is not necessary continually to urge it on.[21]

The removal of Röhm had become unavoidable, but Hitler also took the precaution of eliminating in·the "Night of the Long Knives" perhaps as many as four hundred of his critics from outside the S.A. On Hindenburg's death Hitler could become, without any opposition, the Führer of the German Reich. The army appeared to have saved itself from Röhm, and in gratitude it swore allegiance to Hitler:

Unconditional obedience to the Führer of the German Reich and people, Adolf Hitler, the Supreme Commander of the Wehrmacht . . .[22]

How Nazi Germany was governed

ALTHOUGH NAZI PROPAGANDA created the impression of an efficient state, behind the scenes the administration of Germany was chaotic. Hitler governed Germany through a policy of divide and rule. In 1933 he kept on the civil service, the existing ministries and the local government officials, but they were usually duplicated by Nazi officials and specially created Nazi policy groups. The result was rivalry and contradictory decisions.

The main role of the Nazi party, which was supposed to be an elite of only about 10 percent of the population, was to control and brainwash the Germans. This was done indirectly through such organizations as the Hitler Youth and the German Labor Front, which were controlled by the party. There was also a system of "block leaders," who reported back regularly to their local party bosses on the people in their apartments, streets or villages. One German later recalled:

It was considerably more difficult to keep a secret from one's often harmless block leader, who was obliged to report all his observations, than to mislead the Gestapo.[23]

A block leader because he was close to the people could easily gather a great deal of information.

The Nazi party was split from top to bottom by internal rivalries. The Nazi leaders fought for Hitler's attention, and the Gauleiters competed against each other as if they were medieval barons trying to enlarge their lands.

The reason why Nazi Germany did not collapse from its own contradictions lies partly in the fact that Hitler allowed the experts in the civil service, army and industry to continue their work. Hitler's power was underpinned by the much-feared Gestapo, and by the S.S., both of which were controlled by Himmler. In July 1934 the S.S. was made independent of the S.A., and from then on became a Nazi elite force. Its notorious Death's Head units policed the concentration camps, and the *Waffen-S.S.* became the fighting arm of the organization, which in time was to be a greater threat to the generals than ever the S.A. had been.

Stormtroopers enrolled as auxiliary policemen round up political opponents to Hitler. The S.A. (or Brownshirts) were the Nazi party's original bodyguards. The much-feared S.A. and S.S. underpinned Hitler's hold on Germany.

In the final analysis it was Hitler himself who kept Nazi Germany together. Only he as Führer could make peace among the rival Nazi groups. The Nazi propaganda machine also made sure that his all-powerful image reached every citizen in the Reich. In November 1939 a Nazi district leader in Wiesbaden observed that:

> *His [Hitler's] person forms the main link between the party and the people. One has to recognize that we have a long way to go before the party as such is firmly rooted in the people.*[24]

It was the force of Hitler's personality rather than party policy that won him support.

▶ **A propaganda poster for the S.A., showing an S.A. man striding past cheering youths and turning his back on capitalism and the Church.**

▼ **Units of the Hitler Youth on parade at a summer camp in 1934. Boys were taught sports, war games and Nazi ideology.**

The Jews

To many Germans of Hitler's generation the Jews, who formed about 1 percent of the population, seemed to be destroying all the old traditional values of Germany. Jews seemed to be either great industrialists destroying small businessmen, or Communists planning revolution, or intellectuals challenging all that was old and sacred. They had indeed gone into politics, business, university teaching and journalism because up to 1918 they were banned from the top posts in the civil service, the officer corps and the judiciary.

It was easy to blame them for everything that had gone wrong since 1914. They became a scapegoat for Germany's misfortunes. Hitler shared this view, and hated the Jews with an intensity that few Germans could rival. His frequently declared aim was "to rescue Germany from the Jew who is ruining our country."[25] However, although many Germans were hostile to Jews, it did not necessarily mean they would condone their murder.

Jewish stores were attacked in 1933, but the threat of an international trade boycott soon persuaded Hitler temporarily to tolerate Jewish businesses in the interests of the wider German economy. However, Jews were expelled from the civil service and banned from higher education and the media. In 1935, in response to growing pressure from the party, Hitler introduced the Nuremberg Laws, which deprived the Jews of German citizenship and banned marriages between Jews and gentiles.

By 1938 the German economy was much stronger, and Austria had been successfully

A poster advertising the anti-Semitic film *The Eternal Jew*. It shows the Jew as a combination of evils: moneylender, Bolshevik and slave-driver.

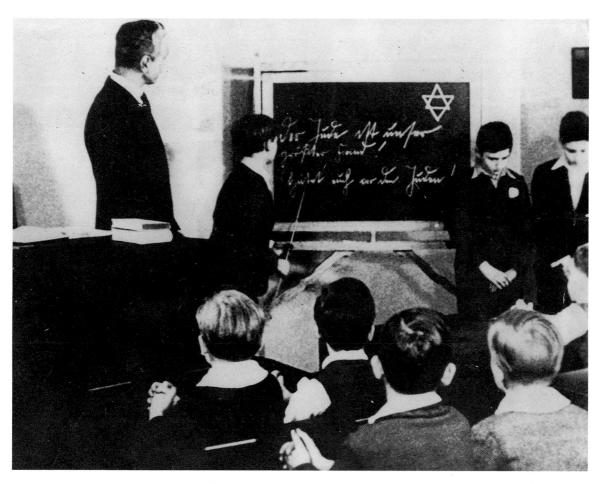

Two Jewish boys have been called out in front of the class. Behind them on the blackboard is written: "The Jew is our greatest enemy. Beware of the Jew." Incidents such as this regularly occurred in schools throughout the Reich.

annexed. Hitler could now quicken the pace of his anti-Semitic policies without fear of foreign protests. There followed in rapid succession a series of government measures that were aimed at segregating the Jews still further and at taking over their businesses and property.

The murder of Ernst von Rath, the German diplomat, in Paris on November 7, 1938 by a 17-year-old Jewish student provided the excuse for the ferocious night of riots, *die Kristallnacht*, in which Nazi mobs were given a free hand to burn down synagogues and loot Jewish property. In January the S.S. was authorized by Goering to set up a Reich Central Office for Jewish Emigration for those Jews lucky enough to be able to buy exit visas. Hitler made it very clear what would happen to those left behind:

Today I will once more be a prophet: if the international financiers in and outside Europe should succeed in plunging the nations into a world war, then the result will not be bolshevization of the earth and thus the victory of Jewry, but the annihilation of the Jewish race in Europe.[26]

Imagine how a Jewish person must have felt in Nazi Germany in early 1939.

Education, youth and culture

The philosophy of Nazism was based on a belief in German racial superiority and in war as an ennobling experience for mankind. University and school teachers were expected to reflect these attitudes in the classrooms and lecture rooms. Apart from a small number of so-called elite Nazi colleges, the Napolas and the Adolf Hitler Schools, the school system was unchanged. However, in the syllabuses much more emphasis was placed on physical education, biology, German and history, as these subjects could easily be twisted into giving students a one-sided picture of German racial and cultural superiority. Nazi ideology was less successful in influencing science and mathematics, but even here it could often make its views felt. In one school mathematics textbook, for example, the following

Propaganda was aimed even at the very young children. This picture is from an elementary school reading book published in 1934. It presents the Hitler Youth as fun and innocent.

question was set:

> *A modern night bomber can carry 1,800 incendiaries. How long (in kilometers) is the path along which it can distribute these bombs, if it drops a bomb every second at a speed of 250 kilometers per hour?*[27]

The students were being brainwashed into accepting the inevitability of war.

Further indoctrination took place in the Hitler Youth, which became compulsory for both sexes in 1939. Boys were taught a mixture of sports, war games and Nazi ideology, while girls studied home economics in the League of German Girls. Biased teaching and the interruption of classes and homework by Hitler Youth activities led to a decline in pupils' school performances. Commenting on the low standard of recruits for the army, one colonel said:

> Our Youth starts off with perfectly correct principles in the physical sphere of education, but frequently refuses to extend this to the mental sphere . . . Many of the candidates for commissions display a simply inconceivable lack of elementary knowledge.[28]

The narrow focus of Nazi education led to a decline in educational standards.

Like the teachers, artists, writers and architects had to follow the Nazi line. Painters and sculptors concentrated on producing groups of Nordic peasants, soldiers or large, unsexy, female Germanic nudes, while architects designed pompous buildings in the Roman imperial style. Modern art was regarded as decadent and removed from public galleries. All debate and experiments were banned, as the following comments in a German paper, *The Simplicissimus*, showed:

> There were times when one went to exhibitions and discussed whether the pictures were rubbish . . . Now there are no more discussions – everything on the walls is art and that is that.[29]

▲ A parade of Hitler Youth in Nuremberg stadium on the annual Nazi Party Day, 1933. Such parades mirrored those of the S.S. and the Wehrmacht.

◄ A German recruiting poster, 1944, announcing that 17-year-olds were to be called up to serve in the armed services. A halo of light seems to protect the boys from any danger.

The role of women

Nazi ideology had very definite ideas about the role of women in society. At the Nuremberg rally in 1934 Hitler described it as follows:

> *If one says that man's world is the state, his struggle, his readiness to devote his powers to the service of the community, one might be tempted to say that the world of women is a smaller world. For her world is her husband, her family, her children and her house. But where would the greater world be if there were no one to care for the small world? . . . Providence has entrusted to women the cares of that world which is peculiarly her own . . . Every child that a woman brings into the world is a battle waged for the existence of her people.[30]*

Hitler saw women's role in society as restricted to that of wife and mother.

The Nazi government tried hard to discourage women from working, unless they were helping their husbands on the land. Women were banned from becoming members of the Reichstag or from the higher posts in the legal profession. They were also stopped from serving on juries because they were allegedly unable to "think logically or reason objectively, since they are ruled only by emotion."[31]

In 1933 married women doctors and civil servants were dismissed. The number of girls studying in higher education was also drastically reduced. Only within the Women's Sections of the party could ambitious Nazi women make a career.

The government tried to persuade women

A factory producing radios for the Ministry of Propaganda. The radio was used by Goebbels for spreading mass propaganda.

In idealizing the German mother, the Third Reich relegated women to the kitchen and the pains of childbirth – it was considered a women's duty to produce four children by a racially pure German man in order to maintain the great German Empire the Reich was hoping to establish.

to give up working in the factories and offices by making marriage financially attractive by offering generous loans, maternity grants and family allowances. At first the government had some successes, but it was trying to challenge an inevitable trend. Since 1914 women had increasingly begun to move into the workplace in all modern industrial societies.

Not surprisingly the Nazis failed in their campaign to keep women at home. Many employers preferred them to men because they were paid less. By 1937, when it was already becoming difficult to find workers, industry began to recruit women to work in the new factories set up under the Four-Year Plan. The government found itself forced to give up its earlier rule that only unemployed women could receive marriage loans.

Nazi propaganda reluctantly accepted women's working in industry. A female propagandist wrote in 1940:

> It has always been our chief article of faith that woman's place is in the home – but since the whole of Germany is our home we must serve her wherever we can best do so.[32]

Through careful wording, the Nazis had changed the accepted role of women from housewife to factory worker.

An economic survey 1933–39

HITLER'S IMMEDIATE PRIORITY, after he had made his own position safe in March 1933, was to create jobs for the unemployed. More than a billion marks were spent on various job-creation projects: canals were dug, housing developments built and a network of new expressways was begun, which provided work for thousands in the building and engineering industries. Money was offered to industry and even to homeowners for additions and repairs.

All this helped restore business confidence and led to a big expansion in production at a time when the world was beginning to recover from the depression. A further million unemployed young people were drafted into the Labor Service and Emergency Relief programs. Rearmament, which created many new jobs, helped Hitler to reduce unemployment almost to nothing by 1939.

Table showing the number of unemployed people in Germany between 1933 and 1939.

(In millions)

Year	January	July
1933	6.042	5.392
1934	3.773	2.426
1935	2.974	1.754
1936	2.520	1.170
1937	1.853	0.563
1938	1.052	0.218
1939	0.302	0.038

33

The table above shows the dramatic decrease in the number of unemployed between 1933 and 1939.

Krupp's steelworks in the Ruhr, 1934. The increased production of steel was a vital part of Hitler's plan to revitalize industry.

A work-creation project under way. Dikes were dug to drain marshlands and reclaim the land. Projects like these reduced unemployment and secured Hitler massive support.

Farmers were helped by the setting up of the Reich Food Estate, a government-controlled office that had the power to fix higher prices for crops so that they could be insulated from the world collapse in food prices. As peasants were seen by Hitler to be "the bloodstock of the German nation," since their children were tough and made good soldiers, they were protected from bankruptcy by the Hereditary Farm Law of October 1933, and their ownership of their land was guaranteed by the state forever.

As Hitler needed the support of big business and industry for rearmament, little help was given to the small shopkeeper or craftsman. Schacht, the Economics Minister and president of the *Reichsbank*, was the genius who financed rearmament by persuading the bankers and industrialists to provide much of the money for it. However, Schacht believed that Germany in the long term had to pay for rearmament by increasing its exports. If necessary he was ready to slow down the rearmament program, if Germany did not export enough.

Hitler disagreed with this and countered by drawing up the Four-Year Plan. Its aim was to prepare Germany for war by 1940 by increasing food production and inventing substitutes for oil, rubber and other vital imports. Large plants were built for making rubber and oil substitutes, and an enormous state-controlled steelworks, named after Hermann Goering, was built. Although production increased greatly, Germany did not become self-sufficient and was not economically ready for total war in 1940.

The workers

If industrial production was not to be threatened by rising wages and strikes, it was vital for the Nazi regime to keep a tight grip on the workers. The trade unions were replaced by the Labor Front in 1933, and Reich Trustees of Labor were put in charge of fixing wages and keeping the factories strike free. As far as possible, the government tried to freeze wages at their low level of 1931–32. But such measures were not popular with German workers; Hitler needed other methods to maintain control.

Potentially the workers formed the strongest block of opposition to the Nazis. Hitler needed to win, at the very least, their toleration. Full employment helped, but he also tried to give them the impression that they were a valued and important group in a Reich where there were no longer class divisions. In a famous speech on Labor Day (May 1), 1937, Hitler claimed:

> *We in Germany have really broken with a world of prejudices . . . I, too, am a child of the people; I do not take my line from any castle: I come from the workshop. Neither was I a general. I was simply a soldier, as were millions of others. It is something wonderful that among us an unknown from the army of the millions of German people – of workers and of soldiers – could rise to be head of the Reich and of the nation.*[34]

The Labor Front had a special section, called the Beauty of Work, that tried to make factories more humane by putting in

A poster advertising the new Volkswagen. The slogan reads: "You must save 5 marks a week if you want to drive your own car." The outbreak of war prevented the program from taking off.

new lighting, improving cafeterias and building swimming pools for the workers. Another section of the Labor Front organized bargain package vacations for the workers, while plans were drawn up for building a cheap people's car (the Volkswagen) and for a savings system that would help people to pay for it.

The workers may have been impressed with all this but it certainly did not stop them from demanding higher wages once employers were short of labor. On the other hand, Hitler's propaganda clearly had some impact. A report from an illegal Social

▼ An advertisement for the Volksempfänger, or people's receiver (radio). The caption says: "All Germany hears the Führer on the Volksempfänger." This was another of the Nazis' effective methods of reaching the workers with propaganda.

Kraft durch Freude

Auch Du kannst jetzt reisen!

Besorge Die noch heute eine Reisekarte der NSG 'Kraft durch Freude'. Der KdF-Wart Deines Betriebes und folgende Stellen geben sie kostenlos aus: Bank der Deutschen Arbeit, alle öffentlichen Sparkassen, Genossenschaftskassen (DGV und Raiffeisen) Thüringische Staatsbank

▲ One of the Labor Front's posters, advertising the possibilities of travel and vacations for workers – a totally new opportunity for many. This was organized by the "Strength Through Joy" section.

Democratic Party (SPD) underground group in Berlin revealed that:

> . . . For a large number of Germans the announcement of the People's Car came as a pleasant surprise . . . This car psychosis [craze], which has been cleverly induced by the Propaganda Ministry, keeps the masses from becoming preoccupied with a depressing situation.[35]

Certainly, the workers must have been pleased with all the new opportunities and products that had become available to them.

The problems behind rearmament

On March 15, 1938, Hitler staged a two-hour military parade to illustrate the might of Germany's army.

Germany's economic revival was miraculous, but could it last? Hitler wanted to avoid a total war economy with food rationing and shortages of consumer goods such as radios, private cars, clothes and furniture, because this would remind the Germans of the terrible years of 1916–18. He wanted to produce both "guns and butter," to keep the Germans happy with his regime. But by trying to achieve this, he ran the risk of causing a major economic crisis and damaging his rearmament program.

Imports poured into Germany not only because of rearmament but also because millions of workers, who were now earning a regular wage, had more money to spend on consumer goods. Germany was unable to export enough goods to pay for its imports. In 1934 the army began to criticize the Labor Front for not controlling the workers' demands sufficiently. One memorandum sent to Hitler asked:

> *Why is the nation not urged to undergo self-denial and restrictions in order to overcome this economic crisis? The measures of individual leaders of the Labor Front run directly counter to these requirements . . . The Labor Front spends large amounts on buying luxurious houses and similar extravagances.*[36]

Schacht temporarily solved the crisis by the New Plan, which controlled the amount of foreign currency industrialists could spend on imports. He also negotiated new export markets in the Balkans and South America, but by 1935 the situation was as bad as ever.

To make Germany independent of imports, Hitler introduced the Four-Year Plan. The table below right shows the actual industrial output of various commodities between 1936 and 1942 and the targeted production. Few commodities met their production target.

▲ A newly launched fishing boat named after Hitler, April 1933. The plan was to build a whole fleet named after prominent Nazis.

▲ This poster is asking Germans to give money for the construction of Youth Hostels and homes.

Output (in thousands of tons)

	1936	1938	1942	Target
Mineral Oil:	1,973	2,579	6,900	15,245
Buna (artificial rubber):	0.7	5.5	106	132
Aluminum:	108	216	287	301
Hard coal:	174,605	205,205	183,048	235,000

37

Full employment also led to employers' illegally increasing skilled workers' wages, which threatened to put inflationary pressures on the economy. Expenditure on consumer goods increased more in the period 1938–39 than in any other period between 1919 and 1940. This meant that, despite the claims of Nazi propaganda, the German economy was in trouble by 1939. Perhaps one solution was a war of conquest, which, if carried out by a victorious blitzkrieg, would enable the Nazi economy to gain control of foreign armaments production and gold reserves.

Nazi aggrandizement 1933-39

BY 1933 THE ALLIES had evacuated the Rhineland. As a result of the depression, reparations had also been scaled down to almost nothing. So Hitler had considerable freedom of action. In 1933 he withdrew from the League of Nations and in 1934 smashed the French alliance system in eastern Europe by signing a ten-year non-aggression pact with Poland. It was not until the reintroduction of conscription in Germany in 1935, which directly challenged the Treaty of Versailles, that Britain, France and Italy agreed to resist any attempts to use force to break the Versailles peace settlement.

Any chance of united action against Hitler was destroyed, first by Britain's decision to act alone in June 1935 and sign a naval agreement with Germany limiting the German Navy to 35 percent of the British Navy, and second by Mussolini's conquest of Abyssinia in 1935–36. British public opinion forced its government to take the lead in imposing sanctions on Italy. These did not work, but instead pushed Mussolini into

▲ Hitler welcomes back German "volunteers" from Spain. Hitler wanted to prolong the fighting in Spain so as to distract Britain and France from his activities in central Europe.

◄ Hitler's main ally was the Italian dictator Mussolini, known as *Il Duce* (the leader). The similarity of their Fascist and Nazi systems drew them together in 1936 to form the "Axis."

cooperating with Hitler. In March 1936, while Britain and France were distracted by Abyssinia, Hitler was able to break another key clause of the Treaty of Versailles and occupy the demilitarized Rhineland.

The outbreak of the Spanish Civil War in July 1936 made it even more difficult to build up a united front against Nazi Germany. Hitler and Mussolini helped General Franco, while the USSR helped the Republicans. Britain and France kept an uneasy neutrality, fearing the outbreak of a general war in Spain. Hitler was therefore left alone. In March 1938 he annexed Austria without any opposition.

If Hitler had been more patient, Britain and France would almost certainly have been ready to discuss ways of handing over to Germany most of the territory that it had lost at Versailles or in which a large number of German-speaking people lived. This was clearly shown at the Munich Conference in September 1938 where German-speaking Sudetenland was surrendered to Hitler. But Hitler was too impatient and ambitious.

When Hitler invaded Czechoslovakia in March 1939, Britain and France guaranteed Poland against a German attack. Then in an amazing about-face Hitler negotiated a nonaggression pact with the USSR on August 23, 1939. He was now safe from a war on two fronts and could move against Poland, which had flatly refused to return the Danzig Corridor to Germany. German troops attacked on September 1, and on September 3, Britain and France declared war.

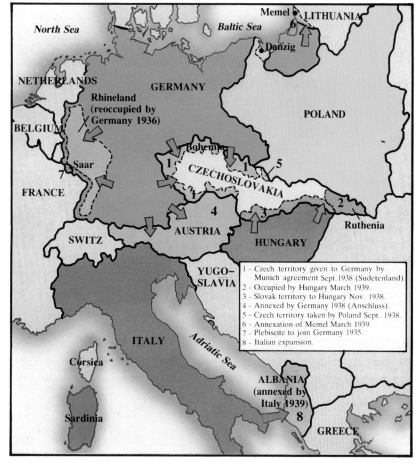

1 - Czech territory given to Germany by Munich agreement Sept. 1938 (Sudetenland)
2 - Occupied by Hungary March 1939.
3 - Slovak territory to Hungary Nov. 1938.
4 - Annexed by Germany 1938 (Anschluss).
5 - Czech territory taken by Poland Sept. 1938.
6 - Annexation of Memel March 1939.
7 - Plebiscite to join Germany 1935.
8 - Italian expansion.

This map shows the spread of German and Italian power into central Europe, 1934–39. Hitler's expansionist policy came first from his nationalistic desire to regain land lost by the Treaty of Versailles, and second from ambitions to gain *lebensraum*.

Austria and Czechoslovakia

Historians cannot agree on what the aims of Hitler's foreign policy were. Some argue that Hitler's priority after smashing the Versailles settlement was to defeat the USSR and gain space for expansion in the Ukraine. Others say he wanted to dominate Europe and set up a German world empire. One historian, A.J.P. Taylor, surprised everybody when he argued:

> *In my opinion statesmen are too absorbed by events to follow a preconceived plan. They take one step and the next follows from it.*[38]

In other words, he believed Hitler had no particular plan apart from making Germany

March 9, 1938, Schussnig, the Austrian Chancellor, announcing plans for a plebiscite in support of "a free and German Austria, an independent and socially-just Austria, a Christian and United Austria."

great again. But at the meeting in the Reich Chancellery on November 5, 1937, Hitler laid down a clearly stated program for action.

> *The aim of German policy was to make secure and to preserve the racial community and to enlarge it. It was therefore a question of space . . .*

Therefore, the question for Germany was where could it achieve the greatest gain at the lowest cost.

> . . . Nobody knew today what the situation would be in the years 1943–45. One thing was certain, that we could wait no longer.[39]

Hitler expected a war against Britain and France by 1945, but was ready to annex Austria and Czechoslovakia in 1938 if there were any chance of success.

Hitler had long wanted the Anschluss with Austria, but the chance came unexpectedly when the Austrian Chancellor, Schussnig, visited Hitler to discuss halting the activities of the Austrian Nazis. Hitler immediately dictated an agreement that would have made Austria a German satellite. When Schussnig later tried to drop it, Hitler sent in troops and annexed the country, because he could not risk a damaging failure.

Hitler planned his policy toward Czechoslovakia more carefully. Because of its alliance with France he regarded it as a "French aircraft carrier" in central Europe. He therefore set October 1 as a deadline for "smashing" Czechoslovakia. Britain's intervention at Munich forced Hitler to cancel the attack, but new plans were quickly drawn up. Hitler also encouraged the Slovaks to demand independence from the Czechs, so that the unity of Czechoslovakia would be broken. On March 14, 1939 Hitler pushed the Slovaks into breaking away and then occupied the whole of Czechoslovakia.

▼ The British Prime Minister, Neville Chamberlain, arrives back on September 16, after his first meeting with Hitler on the Sudeten crisis. Chamberlain believed he could meet German grievances by direct discussions with Hitler.

▼ A cartoon from the British magazine, *Punch*, of the Munich conference. From left to right: Mussolini, Daladier, Chamberlain and Hitler.

FOUR'S COMPANY

All together. "Well, before we go on, here's to Self-sacrifice!"

The outbreak of war, 1939

A famous cartoon on the Nazi–Soviet Pact of August 23, 1939. Despite being leaders of enemy regimes, Stalin and Hitler somehow managed to come to an agreement.

Before Hitler could declare war on either the USSR or the Western powers, he needed to know how Poland would react. In January he tried, in vain, to persuade the Poles to agree to the return of Danzig to the Reich. When Britain and France guaranteed Poland against a German attack on March 31, Hitler immediately ordered preparations for an attack on Poland any time after September 1, 1939. Was he preparing for a general war, or did he believe that Britain and France would back down? On May 23 he told his generals that:

> *There is . . . no question of sparing Poland, and the decision remains to attack Poland at the first suitable opportunity.*
>
> *We cannot expect a repetition of Czechoslovakia. There will be war. The task is to isolate Poland.*[40]

He hoped that France and Britain would not fight, but was ready to risk war if they did stand by Poland.

Throughout the summer Hitler put pressure on Poland by demanding the return of Danzig and the Corridor. On August 23 Ribbentrop, the German Foreign Minister, signed the Nazi–Soviet Pact. In return for being given eastern Poland, the USSR would remain neutral if war broke out between Germany and Poland and its Western allies. This move was certainly an about-face for Hitler. Only three years earlier he had written:

Germany will as always have to be regarded as the focus of the Western World against the attacks of Bolshevism . . . At the moment there are only two countries in Europe which can be regarded as standing firm against Bolshevism – Germany and Italy.[41]

Hitler hoped that news of this pact would isolate Poland. German troops invaded on September 1, but Hitler was unpleasantly surprised by the British ultimatum that followed two days later. Hitler's interpreter recalled:

There was complete silence, Hitler sat motionless, gazing before him . . . After an interval . . . he turned to Ribbentrop with a savage look, as though implying that his foreign minister had misled him about England's probable reaction.
[Next door] . . . Goebbels stood in a corner downcast . . . Everywhere in the room I saw looks of grave concern.[42]

Polish soldiers captured in the early days of the war being marched off by German troops to a prisoner-of-war camp.

War and defeat

UP TO DECEMBER 1941 the German Army won an unbroken series of victories. Poland was easily isolated and defeated in six weeks. Thanks to the Nazi–Soviet Pact the British naval blockade had little impact on the German economy. So, in the spring of 1940 Hitler was able to launch a lightning attack on France, which forced the French to surrender on June 16 and the British to retreat back across the English Channel. Italy entered the war on the German side in June. Hitler hoped that Britain would now come to terms with Germany. He was surprised by Prime Minister Churchill's determination to fight on, but decided on July 31, 1940 to attack the USSR the following spring. Hitler told his generals that the defeat of the USSR was necessary since Britain was only fighting on in the hope that the USSR would come to its aid.

In fact it was his long-term ambition to destroy the USSR. At first he seemed to be successful, but when the Russians halted the Germans near Moscow in December 1941, Hitler realized that he had a long war on his hands. The European war became a world war when Japan attacked the U.S. naval base at Pearl Harbor. To encourage the Japanese, Hitler immediately declared war on the United States. He hoped that the U.S. would be too busy in the Pacific fighting Japan to help Britain in Europe.

At home the production of armaments was increased. Albert Speer set up a Central

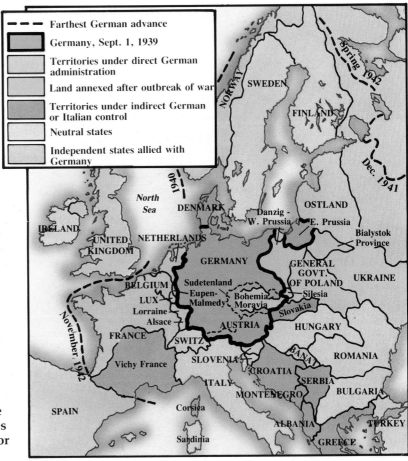

Europe at the height of Nazi power, 1942. The sheer scale of Axis triumphs, however, left them over-extended, fighting on too many fronts and defending too many territories at a time when the balance of men and resources were beginning to tip in favor of the Allies.

Map legend:
- Farthest German advance
- Germany, Sept. 1, 1939
- Territories under direct German administration
- Land annexed after outbreak of war
- Territories under indirect German or Italian control
- Neutral states
- Independent states allied with Germany

▼ A cartoon depicting Hitler as a crazed man-eater devouring Europe.

▲ Soviet bombers over Berlin, 1945. Heavy bombing contributed to the breakdown of German morale.

Planning Board, which was so efficient that the German war economy reached its peak in 1944, despite the Allied bombing campaign. In January 1943 Hitler reluctantly agreed to the conscription of women to work in the factories to replace the men called up to fight. Millions of foreign workers were also forcibly deported from Nazi-occupied Europe to work in Germany.

By 1943 Germany was in retreat. The Afrika Korps had been defeated at El Alamain and, more important, the German 6th Army had been destroyed at Stalingrad. By the summer of 1944 the ring was closing: Allied bombers pounded German cities, the USSR reached Warsaw, and Anglo-American forces landed in France. Any separate German peace with the West was impossible because the Allies had agreed to fight on until Germany surrendered unconditionally. Only the occupation of Germany itself in 1945 brought about peace.

The "final solution"

A boat-load of Jews lucky enough to emigrate from the Third Reich before all escape routes were cut off by the war.

The grip of the Nazi party tightened on Germany during the Second World War as the need for propaganda and supervision of the population became even more important. Party activists argued that the time had come for a real Nazi revolution. Hitler seemed to agree. He personally ordered the euthanasia ("mercy killing") of handicapped Germans. About 80,000 were killed, but public opinion led by Cardinal von Galen, the Bishop of Münster, forced Hitler to stop the killings.

Although, Hitler stopped the euthanasia, he did not stop the murder of the Jews. The war changed for the worse the position of Jews in Germany. It cut off their escape and made Hitler independent of any moral or economic pressures from abroad. It also put over six million Jews in occupied Europe at the mercy of the Nazis. Mass deportation

of Jews from the Reich to Poland began in the winter of 1939–40.

In preparation for the invasion of the USSR, specially trained "task forces" were formed by the S.S. in April 1941 to execute Jews and Communist officials. In July Goering entrusted Heydrich, Himmler's right-hand man, with the task of preparing the "final solution," as the mass murder of six million Jews was so misleadingly called. Experiments with a lethal cyanide gas, called Zyklon B, took place in a concentration camp at Auschwitz. The final details were worked out at the Wannsee Conference in Berlin on January 20, 1942, where Heydrich reported:

In the process of the final solution, the Jews will be conscripted for labor in the eastern territories . . . Large labor gangs of those fit for work will be formed, with the sexes separated, which will be sent to those areas for road construction, and undoubtedly a large number of them will drop out through natural elimination. The remainder who survive – and they will certainly be those who have the greatest powers of endurance – will have to be dealt with accordingly . . .

In the process of carrying out the final solution, Europe will be combed through from west to east . . .[43]

In 1942 the death camps at Auschwitz, Sobibor, Majdanek, Treblinka and elsewhere began their work of mass extermination of the Jews in earnest. So important was this work to the Nazis that trains taking Jews to the death camps took precedence over army supply trains that were going to the front. By the end of World War II in 1945 almost six million Jews had been murdered.

▲ The intense suffering and degradation of Russian and Polish Jews in a concentration camp.

▼ Jews on their way to "resettlement" in Poland in 1940–41. Many probably ended up in concentration camps.

Did a German opposition exist?

When the concentration camps were liberated in 1945, the world asked why the Germans had not done more to overthrow the Nazi regime. Opposition groups had existed, but they were weak and isolated. They operated in a society that accepted Hitler as a man who had restored full employment and national unity. The majority of Germans who opposed Hitler belonged to "the silent opposition."[44] That meant that some of the bravest of them hid Jews from the Gestapo – about 5,000 Jews were hidden in private houses in Berlin; others might listen to BBC radio broadcasts or crack anti-Nazi jokes, such as this one:

A Berliner and a Viennese exchange air raid reminiscences. The former says, "The raid was so heavy that for hours after the all-clear window panes were hurtling down into the street."
"That's nothing. In Vienna, portraits of the Führer were raining down into the street for days after the raid."[45]

But this did not present any serious opposition to the Nazis.

If a German wanted to smash the Nazi regime, there was little he or she could do. Workers' groups and student opposition were quickly broken up by the Gestapo. The only organizations independent enough to criticize Hitler openly were the Church and army, but neither of these ever came out in

Former S.S. camp guards carrying dead bodies from trucks to a communal grave under supervision of British troops at Belsen, April 1945.

total opposition to the Nazis. Both Protestant and Catholic bishops wanted to protect their churches from persecution, but many individual priests like the Lutheran Dietrich Bonhoeffer or the Catholic priest Alfred Delp showed great courage in their stand against Hitler. Nearly 400 Protestant priests died in Buchenwald concentration camp, as did countless other Germans.

The army had the power to destroy Hitler. In September 1938 a group of high-ranking generals drew up a plan to have Hitler arrested and to hold free elections if war were to break out, but Hitler's success at Munich forced them to cancel it. Hitler's brilliant successes of 1939–41 made opposition even more difficult. It was not until 1943 that opposition groups on both the Right and Left united behind a plan drawn up by Colonel Claus von Stauffenberg to assassinate Hitler by planting a bomb in his headquarters. His fellow conspirator General von Treschkow argued that:

> The assassination must be attempted at any cost. Even should it fail . . . we must prove to the world and to future generations that the men of the German Resistance dared to take the decisive step and to hazard their lives upon it. Compared with this object nothing else matters.[46]

For von Treschkow it was important to carry out this plan in order to show the world that German opposition did exist.

The bomb went off but failed to kill Hitler. The conspirators were arrested, and Germany's last chance before defeat to rid itself of the Nazis had passed.

► **Goering points out the damage done by Stauffenberg's bomb to the Conference Room in the Führer's headquarters at Rastenburg, on July 20, 1944. A stenographer was killed outright and three officers later died of wounds. In revenge Hitler had 5,000 people who were involved in the plot executed by April 1945.**

▲ **A German woman branded as a friend of the Jews. The placard on her says: "I am the greatest swine in town and only mix with Jews."**

The collapse of Nazi Germany

By the autumn of 1944 there was no way in which Germany could win the war. Bombing had cut vital oil supplies and damaged the rail network so seriously that it was almost impossible to keep factories supplied with raw materials. Everywhere there was chaos and destruction. Still, the mass of the German people did not do what they did in November 1918: revolt against the continuation of the war. One German writer wrote in despair in his diary:

You, my readers, who will have these lines before your eyes only at some later time, can you grasp it, that such a thing was possible? That our German people in all calmness – Yes in all calmness, that is, without the majority even doing any serious grumbling about it – looked on, while a pack of fools, against whom destiny has long since decided, let the whole wonderful Reich be transformed into one single garbage heap?[47]

The truth was that the Germans had no option. They knew that neither the USSR nor the Western Allies would stop until they had occupied the whole country. They also knew that the victors would enforce a peace so harsh that the Treaty of Versailles would seem mild in comparison. Hitler summed up this mood when he told Speer:

Even the worst idiot realizes that his house will never be rebuilt unless we win. For that reason alone, we'll have no revolution this time.[48]

The Germans had much to fear from an Allied and Russian victory.

In 1945 many cities in Germany were devastated after years of Allied bombing had reduced them to rubble. This picture of the center of Frankfurt shows the enormity of the damage it suffered.

▲ **Field-Marshal Montgomery of the British Army reads over the surrender pact of the German armed forces in the west, May 5, 1945.**

▼ **Hitler the warlord. In reality, by 1944 he was a sick and broken man, but he remained in command of the German war machine.**

By April 1945 the end had almost come. Hitler shot himself in his bunker in Berlin on April 30, and on May 8 all the remaining German armed forces surrendered.

Hitler had destroyed the German Reich. The rivalry between the USSR and the United States, which he hoped would lead to a Soviet–American war in time to save the Third Reich, in fact tore Germany apart. As a result of the hostility between the two superpowers two different Germanys were set up in 1949.

In the short term, Hitler humiliated his country and led the civilized world to regard Germans as barbarians. In the long term, however, the scale of Hitler's defeat enabled the Germans, in West Germany at any rate, to rebuild a democracy on foundations that are much firmer than those of 1919. Hitler's defeat destroyed forever the power of the old military conservative establishment that had brought down the Weimar Republic.

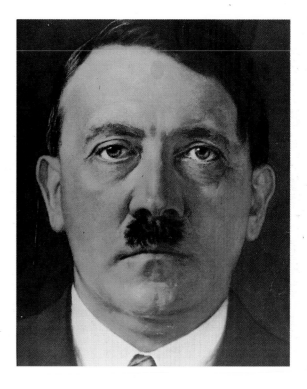

Leading figures

Goebbels, Joseph (1897–1945)

His parents were working-class Catholics in the Rhineland. He joined the Nazi party in 1922. He was a skilled agitator and rabble-rouser. In 1929 Hitler appointed him the party's Reich Propaganda Leader and in 1933 Minister for Public Entertainment and Propaganda. His speech at Munich to the party leaders on November 9, 1938 gave the signal for the *Kristallnacht* riots. During the period 1939–45 he played a major part in maintaining German morale as Minister of Propaganda. He committed suicide on May 1, 1945.

Goering, Hermann (1893–1946)

He was a brilliant air ace in the First World War. He was elected to the Reichstag as a Nazi in 1927. In 1933 he joined Hitler's cabinet as Prussian Minister of the Interior and played a key role in the seizure of power, January to June 1933, as he controlled the Prussian police force. In 1935 he was appointed Commander-in-Chief of the Air Force and in 1936 put in charge of the Four-Year Plan. He played a leading part in Nazi foreign and home policy until the failure of the *Luftwaffe* to stop the Allied bombing of Germany discredited him. He committed suicide in 1946 while awaiting execution at Nuremberg.

Hess, Rudolf (1894–1987)

After fighting in the war he joined the Nazi party in 1920. From 1925 to 1932 he was Hitler's private secretary. In April 1933 he became Deputy Führer. He seemed to be completely loyal to Hitler and incapable of independent action. His sudden flight to Britain in 1941 in an eccentric bid for peace was a great surprise. The British imprisoned him. In 1946 he was sentenced to life imprisonment and was kept in Spandau prison in West Berlin until his death.

Heydrich, Reinhard (1904–1942)

Heydrich was a former naval officer who joined the Nazis in 1931. He became an S.S. general in 1934, and in 1939 was in charge of the Reich's main security office, which included the Gestapo, and in 1941 was entrusted by Goering to organize the "final solution." He became Deputy Reich Protector of Bohemia and Moravia, where he was assassinated on May 27, 1942.

Himmler, Heinrich (1900–1945)

He was the son of a teacher and studied agriculture. He was acting propaganda leader of the Nazi party, 1925–30, and in 1929 became head of the 200-strong S.S., which he expanded to 52,000 by 1933. He organized the Nazi Security Service, and by 1936 was in charge of the criminal and political police in Germany. He planned the details of the purge of June 30, 1934, which, by weakening the S.A., opened the way for the rise of the S.S. The S.S. became a racial elite with responsibility not only for eliminating the Jews but also for creating German settlements in eastern Europe. As Reich Commissioner he was able to resettle Germans from the Baltic territories in Poland and transport Poles and Jews eastward. He did more than any other Nazi to carry out "the final solution." In 1943 he was appointed Minister of the Interior, and, after the July 1944 plot to kill Hitler discredited the generals, he was made Commander-in-Chief of the Army Group Vistula. After trying unsuccessfully to negotiate peace with the U.S., he killed himself after being arrested by the British on May 23, 1945.

Hindenburg, Paul von (1847–1934)

In 1916 he became Supreme Commander of the German armies. In 1925 he was elected President of the Weimar Republic and re-elected in April 1932. On January 30, 1933 he was persuaded by von Papen to appoint Hitler as Chancellor.

Hitler, Adolf (1889–1945)

He was born in Braunau in Austria on April 20, 1889. His father was a 52-year-old customs official and his mother a young peasant girl. He failed to gain a place to study art at the Viennese Academy of Fine Arts. After spending "five years of misery and woe" in Vienna, he moved to Munich in 1913, and in 1914 enlisted in a Bavarian regiment. He left the army to join the German Workers' Party in 1919, and by 1921 was "the Führer" of the movement. During his imprisonment in 1924 Hitler dictated *Mein Kampf* to Rudolf Hess. This book became the "bible" of the Nazis and provided insight into his ideas. It contains his thoughts on political organization and propaganda, shows his hatred and fear of the Jews and outlines his future plans for the destruction of the Versailles Treaty and the colonization of western USSR for German *lebensraum*. It also reveals certain contradictions in Nazi thinking. On the one hand Hitler wanted to return to the "good old days" before the industrial revolution when there were only small farms and workshops. On the other hand his plans to wage war on France and the USSR meant that the Nazis would need the latest technology in industry and science. In 1933 Hitler led the movement to electoral success. On the death of Hindenburg in August 1934 Hitler became both Führer and Chancellor of the German Reich – positions he held until his death on April 30, 1945.

Ribbentrop, Joachim von (1893–1946)

He was the owner of a wine export firm. He joined the Nazi party in 1932 and became Hitler's adviser on foreign policy. After serving as German Ambassador in Britain, he became Foreign Minister. He was hanged at Nuremberg in 1946.

Röhm, Ernst (1887–1934)

He was a regular army captain until 1923, when he was dismissed for his part in the Munich Putsch. After spending two years in Bolivia as a military instructor he took command of the S.A. in 1930 and built it up to a membership of 4½ million by 1933. To Röhm, the S.A. was the most important part of the Nazi movement. He therefore felt betrayed by Hitler's support for the existing army. The resulting tension led to the "Night of the Long Knives."

Schacht, Hjalmar (1877–1970)

Schacht was appointed head of the *Reichsbank* in 1923. He persuaded many bankers and industrialists to support Hitler between 1930 and 1933. He became Minister of Economics in 1934. He then masterminded the financing of German rearmament, but in 1936 he became critical of Hitler's determination to accelerate rearmament even though money was running out. In 1937 he resigned as Minister of Economics and in 1939 was dismissed from the *Reichsbank*. He was arrested by the Nazis in July 1944 on suspicion of plotting against Hitler, but at Nuremberg he was acquitted by the Allies of crimes against humanity.

Speer, Albert (1905–1981)

He was an architect attracted by Hitler's charisma. He planned the design of Nazi rallies and parades after 1933, and was in charge of the Beauty of Labor department of the Labor Front. In 1942 he became Minister of Armaments and War Production and increased output enormously. At Nuremberg he was the only Nazi to acknowledge the evil of the Nazi regime.

Strasser, Gregor (1892–1934)

He was leader of the more socialistic North German branch of the Nazi party. He was critical of Hitler's links with the industrialists between 1930 and 1932. He wanted to join the Schleicher cabinet in December 1932 and resigned from the party when Hitler vetoed this. He was murdered by the Nazis on June 30, 1934.

Important dates

1918
November 9   A republic is declared in Berlin.
November 11 The armistice is signed.

1919
June 28   The Treaty of Versailles signed.
September 16 Hitler joins the German Workers' Party.

1920
February 24 The 25-point program of the National Socialist German Workers' Party.

1921
July 29   Hitler elected chairman of the Nazi party.

1923
January 11   French occupy the Ruhr.
November 8–9 The Munich Putsch.

1924
March 27   Hitler sentenced to five years' imprisonment.
December 23 Hitler released from prison.

1925
February 27 The Nazi party refounded.

1929
October 29   The Wall Street Crash.

1930
March 30   Brüning appointed Chancellor.
September 14 Reichstag election: Nazis win 107 seats.

1932
March–April Presidential election: Hindenburg re-elected.
May 30   Brüning dismissed. Von Papen appointed Chancellor.
July 31   Reichstag election: Nazis win 230 seats.
September 12 Von Papen dissolves the Reichstag.
November 6   Nazis win 196 seats.
December 2   Von Papen resigns and Schleicher appointed Chancellor.

1933
January 30   Schleicher resigns and Hitler appointed Chancellor.
February 27 Reichstag fire.
March 5   Reichstag election: Nazis win 288 seats.
March 23   Enabling Act.
July 14   Law against the formation of new parties.
       Concordat signed with the Vatican.
September 29 Reich Entailed Farm Law.
October   Germany leaves League of Nations.

1934
January 26   Nonaggression pact with Poland signed.
June 30   "Night of the Long Knives."
August 2   Hindenburg dies. Hitler becomes Führer of the German people.
September   The New Plan introduced.

1935
March 16   Conscription reintroduced.

April 11	Stresa meeting.
June 18	Anglo-German naval agreement.
September 15	The Nuremberg Laws concerning Jewish Germans.

1936

March 7	Reoccupation of the Rhineland.
July 17	Spanish Civil War begins.
September	The introduction of the Four-Year Plan.

1937

| November 5 | Important conference on foreign policy. |
| November 26 | Schacht resigns as Minister of Economics. |

1938

February 12	Hitler–Schussnig meeting.
March 12	Invasion of Austria.
May 20	Hitler plans attack on Czechoslovakia.
September	Sudeten crisis.
November 9–10	*Kristallnacht.*

1939

March	Invasion of Czechoslovakia.
March 31	British guarantee to Poland.
May 23	Hitler plans attack on Poland.
August 23	Russo-German Nonaggression Pact.
September 1	Attack on Poland.
September 3	Britain and France declare war.

1940

April	German occupation of Norway.
May–June	Blitzkrieg in France.
June 10	Italy declares war on Britain and France.
July 31	Hitler announces to his generals decision to invade the USSR.
August–September	Battle of Britain.

1941

June 22	German attack on the USSR.
December	German offensive halted outside Moscow.
December 7	Japanese attack on Pearl Harbor.
December 11	German declaration of war on United States.

1942

January 20	Wannsee Conference.
July–January (1943)	Battle of Stalingrad.
October	German defeat at El Alamein.

1943

May	Afrika Korps surrenders.
July	41 U-boats sunk in the Atlantic.
	British and Americans invade Sicily.

1944

| June 6 | D-Day landings. |
| July 20 | Plot against Hitler fails. |

1945

| May 8 | All German forces surrender. |

Glossary

Anschluss	The annexation of Austria in 1938.
Anti-Semite	A person who discriminates against or persecutes Jews.
Blitzkrieg	A lightning war.
Bourgeois	Middle class.
Chancellor	The head of the cabinet in Germany.
Charisma	Strongly magnetic personality by which a leader can attract his or her followers.
Communism	A political and economic theory following the ideas of Karl Marx, who believed in the abolition of all private property and the creation of a classless society.
Constitution	A set of rules and laws according to which a country is governed.
Cosmopolitan	Influenced by ideas from all over the world; not just German.
Danzig Corridor	(Polish Corridor) A narrow tract of land forming a passage to the Baltic Sea; given to Poland in the Treaty of Versailles.
Dawes Plan	The American program devised in 1924 for German reparation payments.
Euthanasia	The act of killing people painlessly, often to relieve them of an incurable illness.
Extremist	Someone who is radical and uncompromising.
Freikorps	"Freecorps" or volunteer forces recruited to defend Germany in December 1918.
Führer	Leader.
Gauleiter	Regional Nazi party leader.
Gestapo	Secret state police.
Gleichschaltung	Coordination or streamlining or putting everything under Nazi control.
Great Coalition	Coalition of the Social Democratic Party and the Center Party that governed Germany from 1928 to 1930.
Hyperinflation	An inflation rate that increases so rapidly that a currency becomes valueless.
Incendiary bomb	A bomb that sets off fires when it explodes.
Indoctrination	To teach people to accept particular opinions and ideas.
Inflation	The increase in the amount of money in circulation; money is less valuable as a result, and prices rise.
Kaiser	Emperor.
KPD	German Communist Party.
Kristallnacht	The anti-Jewish riots of November 9–10, 1938.
Lebensraum	Living space.
Luftwaffe	Air force.
Mark	The German unit of currency.
Mein Kampf	*My Struggle* – the title of the book Hitler wrote.

Nationalism	A strong sense of loyalty and devotion to one's country.
Nonunionized	Not a member of a trade union.
Putsch	A revolt or coup.
Reich	The German state (literally, empire).
Reichsbank	National bank.
Reichskirche	National church.
Reichstag	The lower house of the German parliament from 1871 to 1933.
Reparations	Financial compensation demanded from Germany by the victorious Allies after the First World War.
Republic	A form of government in which power is held by the people or their elected representatives.
Revocation	Cancellation or withdrawal, often of an agreement.
S.A. *(Sturmabteilung)*	Storm or assault troops.
Satellite	A country under the domination of a foreign power.
Scapegoat	Someone who is made to bear the blame for others.
Socialism	An economic theory that believes that the state should own all important means of production and distribution of wealth.
SPD	German Social Democratic Party.
S.S. *(Schutzstaffel)*	Elite guard (protection squad).
Stahlhelm	German First World War veterans' organization.
The Third Reich	Official Nazi name for their regime in Germany. Hitler declared the Third Reich would last for a thousand years. In fact, it lasted only twelve years – from 1933 to 1945.
Total war	War in which the whole of the country's resources are directed toward the war effort.
Trust	A group of industrialists or traders who organize themselves to defeat competition and to control prices.
Waffen–S.S.	Militarized S.S.
Wall Street Crash	The sudden crash in share values on the New York Stock Exchange on October 29, 1929.
Wehrmacht	The German Army.
White-collar workers	Nonmanual workers – those working in stores or offices.

Further reading

Banyard, Peter, *The Rise of the Dictators: 1920–1939*, Franklin Watts, 1986.

Fest, Joachim C., *The Face of the Third Reich*, (Bullock, Michael tr.), Pantheon, 1977.

Grunberger, Richard G., *The Twelve Year Reich*, H. Holt, 1979.

Mosse, George L., *Nazism, A Historical and Comparative Analysis of National Socialism*, Transaction Books, 1978.

Noakes, J. & Pridham, G., *Nazism, 1919–1945*. (2 vols.) A documentary reader, Humanities, 1983, 1984.

Picture acknowledgments

The author and publishers would like to thank the following for allowing their illustrations to be reproduced in this book: E.T. Archive 5 (top), 15 (left), 31 (left), 39 (left); Popperfoto 23 (bottom); Topham Picture Library cover, 7, 9 (bottom), 11, 13, 15 (right), 16, 17, 19, 20, 22 (top), 23, 25, 28, 29, 31 (right), 33, 37 (left), 39 (right), 40 (left & right), 42, 43 (left & right), 44, 45, 47 (top & bottom), 49 (top), 50, 52, 53 (top & bottom); Wayland Picture Library 6, 24, 27 (bottom), 38, 51 (top); Weimar Archive 5 (bottom), 8, 9 (top), 10, 12, 14, 18, 21, 26, 27 (top), 30, 32, 34, 35, 36, 37 (right), 48, 49 (bottom), 51 (bottom). The maps were supplied by Peter Bull.

Notes on sources

1 D.C. Watt, *Hitler's Mein Kampf*, Hutchinson, London, 1969, p. 185.
2 Ed. J. Noakes & G. Pridham, *Documents on Nazism*, Jonathan Cape, London, 1974, pp. 37–9.
3 *Ibid*. p.63.
4 G. Craig, *Germany, 1866–1945*, O.U.P., Oxford, 1978, p. 545.
5 K.D. Bracher, *The German Dictatorship*, Penguin, London, 1973, p. 179.
6 Bruno Gebhardt, *Handbuch der Deutschen Geschichte*, Union Verlag, 1959, p. 352.
7 *Ibid*. pp. 346–7.
8 Craig, *op. cit.* p. 546.
9 Noakes & Pridham, *op. cit.* p. 110.
10 A. Bullock, *Hitler: A Study in Tyranny*, Penguin, London, 1962, p. 217.
11 Noakes & Pridham, *op. cit.* p. 136.
12 *Ibid*. p. 142.
13 Orlow quoted in Williamson, *The Third Reich*, Longman, London, 1982, p. 7.
14 Bracher, *op. cit.* p. 248.
15 Von Papen, *Memoirs*, André Deutsch, London, p. 256.
16 Noakes & Pridham, *op. cit.* p. 161.
17 *Ibid*. p. 193.
18 J.C. Fest, *Hitler*, Penguin, London, 1977, p. 628.
19 Bullock, *op. cit.* p. 281.
20 Craig, *op. cit.* p. 588.
21 Bullock, *op. cit.* p. 299.
22 *Ibid*. p. 309.
23 Ed. J. Noakes, *Government, Party & People in Nazi Germany*, University of Exeter, 1980, p. 28.
24 *Ibid*. p. 28.
25 Bullock, *op. cit.* p. 96.
26 D.G. Williamson, *The Third Reich*, Longman, London, 1982, p. 88.
27 J. Noakes & G. Pridham, *Nazism, 1919–1945*, vol.2, (Exeter Studies no. 8), University of Exeter, 1984, p. 439.
28 Grunberger, *A Social History of The Third Reich*, Penguin, London, 1974, p. 371.
29 *Ibid*. p. 540.
30 Williamson, *op. cit.* p. 85.
31 Grunberger, *op. cit.* p. 331.
32 *Ibid*. p. 328.
33 Williamson, *op. cit.* p. 84.
34 Baynes, ed., *Hitler's speeches*, vol.I. 1922–1939, O.U.P., Oxford, 1942, pp. 620–621.
35 Noakes & Pridham, (*Nazism;* vol. 2), *op. cit.* p. 353.
36 *Ibid*. p. 270.
37 Noakes & Pridham, *op. cit.* p. 412.
38 A.J.P. Taylor, *The Origins of the Second World War*, Hamish Hamilton, London, 1961, p. 69.
39 Extract from *Documents on German Foreign Policy*, (D.G.F.P.) 1918–45, Series D (1933–37), vol.I, H.M.S.O., 1950, pp. 29–38.
40 Noakes & Pridham, *op. cit.* p. 559.
41 Extract from D.G.F.P., Series C., vol. V, no. 490 (6), pp. 854–5.
42 Noakes & Pridham, *op. cit.* pp. 570–571.
43 *Ibid* p. 489.
44 H. Rothfels, *The German Opposition to Hitler* O. Wolff, London, 1973, p. 28.
45 Grunberger, *op. cit.* p. 429.
46 Bullock, *op. cit.* p. 739.
47 Craig, *op. cit.* p. 761.
48 *Ibid*. pp. 761–2.

Index